A GUIDE TO ROME

FIVE WALKING TOURS

P S Quick

Published in 2016 by
Acorn Books
www.acornbooks.co.uk

Acorn Books is an imprint of
Andrews UK Limited
www.andrewsuk.com

Copyright © 2016 P S Quick

The right of P S Quick to be identified as the author of this work has been asserted in accordance with the Copyright, Designs and Patents Act 1998

All rights reserved. No part of this publication may be reproduced, stored in any retrieval system or transmitted in any form or by any means, electronic, mechanical, photocopying, recording or otherwise, without the prior written permission of the copyright holder for which application should be addressed in the first instance to the publishers. No liability shall be attached to the author, the copyright holder or the publishers for loss or damage of any nature suffered as a result of the reliance on the reproduction of any of the contents of this publication or any errors or omissions in the contents.

All information used within this book is believed to be correct at the time of writing. If you find any information within this book that has changed, please advise the publisher who will be happy to correct it in future editions.

Contents

Introduction iv

Preparation v

The First Tour 1

The Second Tour 21

The Third Tour 37

The Fourth Tour 51

The Fifth Tour 63

Final Thoughts 82

Introduction

This book aims to give the tourist an opportunity to visit and enjoy not only the few major attractions that a tour usually includes but also many of the other interesting sights that many people do not see.

By providing five different walking routes and detailed information about each attraction passed, it puts a visitor to Rome in charge of the time spent at any particular place rather than having to rush and keep up with a guide.

With detailed instructions of how to get from one place to another, including the nearest metro stations for the beginning and end of each walking tour, this guide gives a flavour of the many things that Rome has to offer without having to join costly guided tours.

Saint Peter's Square

Preparation

- Before arriving in Rome it advisable to consider which tickets will need to be bought in order to go into attractions. Many of these major sights have long queues just to buy tickets and in the height of the tourist season buying tickets on the day can result in queueing for hours.

- It is possible to buy many tickets on the internet before travelling such as those for the Vatican and Colosseum. Tickets for one attraction, for example the Colosseum, often include free entry to other sights.

- Another option is to buy a *Roma Pass* which, although initially expensive, is worth more than five times its value in the places that can be visited. It also offers priority entrance to attractions and includes metro and bus fares. The price varies according to the number of days for which the pass is valid.

- Do your research on tickets and be careful where you buy. The Roma Pass is probably best bought when you are in Rome as it has a time limit. The pass can be bought in Rome from many museums, tourist points and metro stations.

- Visit a tourist office or kiosk as soon as you can on arrival to pick up details of attractions and opening times together with a free map which is essential in order to get your bearings and understand where places are located.

- The official online tourist office is at: http://www.turismoroma.it/?lang=en This will provide you with details of where the nearest tourist office is to your hotel as well as other information. Hotels usually have free maps for their clients.

- Check opening times and consider the day of the week when choosing a particular walking tour. Some attractions are closed on Mondays although the Capitoline Museums are open every day while the Vatican is closed on Sundays. Often the last admission is one hour before closing time.

- If you want more detailed information than is given in this book you can choose to hire an audio guide for places like the Colosseum. It is also possible to download free audio guides for your iPod or mp3 player from the internet.

- While it is wonderful to sit and enjoy a drink or a meal in the busy piazzas this is often costly and if you are on a budget you will find some good quality competitive restaurants off the main streets. Ask the hotel where the locals eat for the best deals.

- While the walking tours give advice on where to get the metro for travelling around Rome this may not be the best option for you. Some parts of Rome are not close to the metro so a bus may be more appropriate. It is also important to remember that if you walk from one place to another you will see far more than if you travel by public transport.

- If you are walking long distances you need sensible shoes. Rome is built upon seven hills so if you have mobility problems then walking tours may not be suitable as the tourist is often faced with steps or steep roads. If you are fit enough to do it then walking around Rome is rewarding. When visiting churches remember to dress appropriately or you may be refused entry.

The Tours

The First Tour

Today's walk begins at the Piazza Barberini and ends at the Piazza del Popolo. Both of these piazzas have metro stations on Line A.

Main Sights
- Piazza Barberini
- Santi Vincenzo e Anastasio
- Trevi Fountain
- Piazza Colonna
- Tempio di Adriano
- Chiesa di Sant'Ignazio di Loyola
- Piazza Navona
- Pantheon
- Palazzo Altemps
- Iglesia de Sant'Agostino
- Borghese Palace
- Piazza di Spagna
- Spanish Steps
- Piazza del Popolo

Piazza Barberini

The Piazza Barberini is a large square located at the confluence of several streets on the Quirinal Hill. It was named after the Barberini family who made their home here. One of the sons became Pope Urban VIII.

Barberini Palace

The architect Maderno started the construction of the Palazzo Barberini in 1627 but died two years later. Bernini took over and completed it in 1633. The palace still stands in the square and now houses the *Galleria Nazionale d'Arte Antica*, the Museum of Ancient Art. It has a superb collection of Renaissance and Baroque paintings.

Fontana del Tritone

Bernini was also responsible for creating the Baroque Fountain of the Triton for Pope Urban VIII in 1643. Four dolphins are paired and hold a coat of arms, two keys and a papal tiara. The sea god, Triton, sits on one clam shell and sips water from another. The bees on the Barberini coat of arms can also be seen in Saint Peter's Basilica.

Leave Piazza Barberini and walk west along Via del Tritone. After about 350 metres turn left onto Via della Panetteri; walk for 10 metres then straight ahead onto Via della Stamperia. After 210 metres turn left onto Vicolo dei Modelli. After 43 metres you will see the church of St. Vincent and Anastasius.

Santi Vincenzo e Anastasio

This small Baroque church situated near the Trevi fountain was given to the Bulgarian Orthodox Church by Pope John Paul II in 2002. It is worth a visit to see the list of the 22 popes who served from 1583 to 1903 on the left of the altar. Entry is free.

The hearts of these popes still remain in the marble urns kept in this church. It was the custom to remove internal organs to prevent decay while the funeral arrangements were made. The church also contains a large collection of offerings left by people who believed their prayers had been answered.

On leaving the church you will see the Trevi Fountain directly ahead.

Trevi Fountain

The famous Trevi Fountain is the most beautiful fountain in Rome and was featured in Fellini's film *La Dolce Vita*. It is the largest Baroque fountain in Rome and derives its name from *Tre Vie* which refers to the three roads that meet at this point.

It is said that if you throw a coin into the fountain you will definitely return to Rome. Looking away from the fountain the coin should be tossed over the opposite shoulder to the hand holding the coin.

A smaller fountain was built here in the fifteenth century fed by the Agua Virgo, an aqueduct built by Agrippa in 10 BC. In the eighteenth century Pope Clement XII commissioned Nicola Salvi to create a larger fountain to replace it.

The Trevi Fountain

The fountain was built against the wall of the Palazzo Poli and designed like a monumental triumphal arch by Nicola Salvi who was inspired by Bernini's style of architecture. The sea god Neptune stands in the centre riding upon a shell shaped chariot pulled by two horses that represent the changing moods of the sea; one horse restless while the other is obedient. The water flows loudly over the rocks into a large semi-circular basin representing the sea.

Walk west on Piazza di Trevi towards Vicolo del Forno for 18 metres then continue onto Via delle Muratte. After 200 metres turn right onto Via del Corso and after 130 metres left onto Piazza Colonna.

Piazza Colonna

The Piazza Colonna is a square in central Rome just off the main shopping street known as Via del Corso. It takes its name from the huge marble column that stands there and also contains several other important buildings. On the south side is the Palazzo Ferraioli which used to the Papal Post Office. The Palazzo Wedekind stands on the west side of the Piazza and has Roman columns from the ancient city of Veii. The Temple of Marcus Aurelius once stood on this spot. Next to it is the little church of Santi Barolomeo e Alessandro dei Bergamaschi.

Colonna di Marco Aurelio

The Doric Column of Marcus Aurelius built to celebrate the victories of Emperor Marcus Aurelius's military campaigns against the Sarmatians and Germanic tribes was completed in 193 AD.

It is just less than thirty metres tall and built from marble with the spiral reliefs depicting the events that happened during the campaigns. Inside there is a spiral staircase of 201 steps that climb to the top of the column. Originally the statue at the top was of Marcus Aurelius and his wife but in 1589 it was replaced with a statue of Saint Paul.

Palazzo Chigi

The Chigi Palace was completed by Carlo Maderno in 1580 for the Aldobrandini family but bought by the Chigi family in 1659. It is situated on the north side of the plaza and although originally the embassy of Austria-Hungary is now the offices of the Council of Ministers of Italy.

It houses a large collection of sculptures and paintings and is now a museum and cultural centre where exhibitions, concerts, meetings and guided tours are held.

La Fontana di Piazza Colonna

The fountain of the Piazza Colonna can be found in this square. It was commissioned by Pope Gregory XIII and built in 1575 by Giacomo Della Porta and Rocco De Rossi.

Archille Stocchi sculptured two sets of dolphins with entwined tails when the fountain was restored in 1830.

From Piazza Colonna walk to Via dei Bergamaschi and then after 66 metres turn right onto Piazza di Pietra.

Tempio di Adriano

The temple of Hadrian was built to honour the Roman Emperor Hadrian but today houses Rome's Stock Exchange known as the *Borsa Valori di Roma*. Only one row of its eleven columns can now be seen on its north side. A small part of the original temple wall can still be seen behind the columns. It was built by Emperor Antoninus Pius in 145 AD.

Walk east on the Piazza di Pietra towards Via de' Burrò and after 34 metres turn right onto Via de'Burro. After 48 metres keep right to stay on this road. Take a left turn onto Piazza di Sant Ignazio then after 21 metres turn left to stay on Piazza di Sant Ignazio. After 15 metres the church of Saint Ignazio will be on the right.

Chiesea di Sant'Ignazio di Loyola

The Church of Saint Ignazio is a Jesuit church built in 1626 but was only fully completed in 1649. It has a Baroque face designed by Alessandro Algardi. The impressive interior is decorated with marble and stucco. It has magnificent frescos and gilded ornaments as well as funerary monuments of Pope Gregory XV.

The entry of Ignatius into Paradise is depicted on the ceiling which runs the whole length of the nave. Four symbolic figures represent the four continents where the Jesuits hoped to take their religion. An optical illusion tricks the mind into thinking that the once planned dome is really there, although in fact it was never built. A large marble disc stands on the ground to the right of the main entrance marking the place where the spectacular perspective paintings are best viewed.

Walk westwards on Piazza di Sant Ignazio for about 15 metres until you reach Via del Seminario. Continue along this road for another 200 metres onto the Piazza della Rotonda where you will find the Pantheon.

Piazza della Rotonda

The Piazza della Rotonda is today an elegant square but until the end of the nineteenth century was a fish, vegetable and bird market. Today as well as having the magnificent Pantheon on its south side it has a fountain and obelisk.

Pantheon

Before the current Pantheon a temple dedicated to the seven sacred planet gods was built around 25 BC by Marcus Agrippa but when it burned down in 80 BC it was rebuilt by Emperor Domitian. After the building was struck by lighting and burned down again in 110 AD Emperor Hadrian ordered the temple to be rebuilt a second time.

It took seven years to build the new circular temple that remains today as the best preserved temple in Rome. The portico has sixteen huge columns that were quarried in Egypt and transported to Rome. Each is 1.5 metres wide. The amazing dome is 43 metres high and was the highest in the world until Florence Cathedral was built in 1436. The only source of light is the large opening in the dome known as the oculus. The temple became a church in 609 AD. The tomb of Raphael and several Italian kings can be found inside.

Fontana del Pantheon

The Pantheon fountain has changed over the years with the original basin and lions being elevated onto pedestals before being removed. In 1575 Pope Gregory XIII instructed Giacomo Della Porta to rebuild the fountain.

Today it has a large shell raised upon steps of travertine marble with masks and four groups of dolphins. The obelisk of Ramses II was dedicated In 1711 .

Walk to the west of Piazza della Rotunda and turn right onto Via Giustiniani. After about 120 metres cross Via della Dogana Vecchia and continue ahead onto Via del Salvatore. Just less than 100 metres along this road turn left onto Corso del Rinascimiento. You will pass the Madama Palace and the church of Saint Nicholas. Turn right onto Corsia Agonale and right again onto Piazza Navona.

Piazza Navona

Piazza Navona is situated in the heart of historic Rome and often regarded as its most beautiful square. The spectacular Baroque square is surrounded by churches, houses and other buildings as well as three magnificent fountains.

Here you will find street performers, magicians, artists and sellers of souvenirs as well as many restaurants and cafes nearby. Although those around the square are expensive the price paid is well worth the opportunity to sit and enjoy the atmosphere.

In 86 AD the Emperor Domitian organised the building of a stadium known as *Circus Agonalis* which is why the piazza has a long, oval shape. Used for festivals and sporting events it was bigger than the arena of the Colosseum. Although the stadium was paved over in the fifteenth century remnants of it can still be seen and it is possible to join a guided tour of the underground monument.

The Piazza Navona with the Neptune Fountain, the Four Rivers Fountain and Obelisk

Fontana dei Fiumi

The Four Rivers Fountain stands in the middle of the square. It was built for Pope Innocent X between 1647 and 1651. Originally the fountain's design was commissioned by Borromini but eventually given to his rival Bernini as his design was considered more impressive.

A large obelisk which originally stood at the Circus of Maxentius now rises from the centre of the fountain. At each corner stands a statue representing the then longest known rivers from four continents: the Nile, the Ganges, the Danube and the Rio de la Plata.

Fontana del Nettuno

The Neptune Fountain that stands at the northern end of the Piazza Navona was once known as the *Fontana dei Calderari* because it stood near to a small alley where blacksmiths' workshops were located.

The original white marble basin for the fountain was designed by Giacomo Della Porta in 1574 but today's fountain was not completed until 1878 by Antonio della Bitta and Gregorio Zappalà who depicted Neptune fighting with an octopus and sea nymphs with cupids and walruses.

Fontana del Moro

Located at the southern end of Piazza Navona is the Moor Fountain which was designed by Giacomo della Porta in 1575 with four Tritons and a dolphin. Today a statue of a Moor wrestling with a dolphin stands in a conch shell. The statue was created by Bernini.

The original statues are now housed in the Galleria Borghese and the ones on the fountain are copies.

La Chiesa di Sant'Agnese in Agone

The Baroque church of Saint Agnes in Agone was commissioned by Pope Innocent X and designed by Girolamo Rainaldi and his son Carlo in 1652 with the main face, two bell towers and crowned dome being designed by Borromini.

Legend says it was built on the site where the martyr Saint Agnes suddenly grew long hair that preserved her dignity when she was stripped naked. It is believed that she was beheaded here in the third century.

The remains of a Roman mosaic can be seen inside the church as well as a number of large scale sculptures and a shrine containing the skull of Saint Agnes. The main altar has a relief of the Holy Family by Domenico Guidi. The Assumption of Mary frescos were started in 1670 by Ciro Ferri and completed after he died by Sebastiano Corbellini.

Walk to the north of the Piazza Navona and continue onto Via Agonale for about 40 metres before turning right onto Piazza della Cinque Lune then left onto Piazza di Sant'Apolinare where you will find the Pallazo Altemps on the left.

Palazzo Altemps

This beautiful Renaissance palace is now home to a branch of the Museum of Rome and has 33 frescoed halls with some of the best statues in Rome. Girolami Riario started building the palace in 1477 but Riario was assassinated and the palace looted. it was not completed until 100 years later by Cardinal Altemps and remained the property of this family until it was given to the papacy in 1894.

Altemps collected valuable ancient statues and books, some of which remain in the palace. There are over one hundred statues from the seventeenth century by Cardinal Ludovico Ludoviso as well as the Mattei Collection, the Drago Collection and the Egyptian Collection.

One of the most famous exhibits is the outstanding Ludovisi throne from the fifth century which probably depicts the birth of Aphrodite from the sea. There is also the Ludovisi Sarcophagus that portrays battle scenes in its finely carved relief.

The palace even has its own Baroque church know as *Sant'Aniceto del Palazzo Altemps* which has a delightful painted ceiling and the tomb of Saint Anicetus who was pope from 157 AD to 168 AD.

Walk north-east along the Piazza di Sant'Apolinare and turn right onto Via dei Pianellari. After about 50 metres turn right onto the Piazza di Sant'Agostino and the Church of Saint Augustine will be on the right.

Chiesa de Sant'Agostino

The construction of the Church of Saint Augustine was begun in 1296 but was not completed until 1420 with the present Renaissance facade being built by Giacomo di Pietrasanta in 1483. Later restorations in the eighteenth century were by Luigi Vantitelli.

Inside is the sculpture of Mary by Jacopo Sansovino, the famous Baroque painting of Monna di Loreto by Caravaggio, the fresco of the prophet Isaiah by Rafael and a Guercino altarpiece of Saint Agustine, John the Evangelist and Jerome. Among other things the church contains the tomb of Saint Monica, the mother of Augusine.

Walk north on the Piazza di Sant'Agostino and take the Via dei Pianellari then turn right onto Via dei Portoghesi. After 50 metres turn left onto Via della Scofa. After about 170 metres turn right onto Via del Clemention. Continue another 80 metres and turn left onto the Piazza Borghese.

Piazza Borghese

The Piazza Borghese is a square in the historic centre of Rome that was named, like the surrounding area, after the Borghese family who settled here in the sixteenth century.

From the square the western face of the Borghese Palace can be seen. The square was also once called *Piazza delle Catene*, because of the chains placed on the small columns surrounding the entrance. To the right of this facade the Architecture Department of the Sapienza University can be seen.

The square is also the location for the *Mercato delle Stampe* and is worth a visit for its old books, prints, stamps, maps, architectural engravings or music scores among other things. Sit at the cafe in the square and enjoy a drink or an excellent lunch.

Palazzo Borghese

The Borghese Palace built in various stages between 1560 and 1614 was bought in 1604 by Cardinal Camillo Borghese who bequeathed it to his family when he became Pope Paul V in 1605. The palace became the city residence of the Borghese family who still live in part of it today. Their summer residence was the Villa Borghese which is located north of the Piazza del Popolo.

The Borghese family were keen collectors of paintings and antiques. Most of those that were originally in the Palazzo Borghese are today held at the Galleria Borghese. Look out for the eagles and dragons that are the heraldic symbol of this family and decorate many of their properties.

From Piazza Borghese turn left onto Via Borghese and continue onto Largo Fontanella di Borghese. Carry straight on to Largo Carlo Goldoni and Via dei Condotti. After 300 metres turn right onto Piazza di Spagna then after 30 metres turn a sharp left.

Piazza di Spagna

The Spanish Square is one of the busiest, most popular meeting places in Rome and should not to be missed. It takes its name from the Spanish Embassy which has its headquarters in the Palazzo di Spagna in the square. Shelly, Keats and Goethe spent much of their time here and today the Museo Keats-Shelly can be found facing the steps on the right. A long staircase connects the square with a French church that sits on the top of the hill.

Scalinata della Trinità dei Monti

The Spanish Steps commissioned by Pope Innocent XIII in 1723 were designed by the Italian architect Francisco de

Sanctis and completed in 1725. It was financed by the French Ambassador Etienne Gueffier who wanted to connect the French Church with the square. There are twelve different flights with 137 travertine limestone steps in all that form the longest and widest staircase in Europe.

The Spanish Steps with the Fontana della Barcaccia and Trinità dei Monti Church

The elegant staircase looks especially beautiful when it is decorated with flowers. Annually in July the latest fashion creations are modelled on the steps in the moonlight. There is a magnificent view of the square and beyond from the top terrace.

Iglesia Trinità dei Monti

The French Trinity of the Mountains church stands on the top of the hill that overlooks a small square known as Piazza della Trinità dei Monti giving a good view of other parts of the city. A small chapel once existed upon the hill but Charles VIII of France commissioned a new church to be built in 1496.

The Gothic church was plundered during the French Revolution but later restored. It has a Renaissance facade and two cupolas. The chapels inside the church are decorated with paintings that include two by Daniele da Volterra who was one of Michelangelo's pupils. He is also buried in the church.

A giant obelisk stands between the church and the Spanish Steps. It was originally located in the Gardens of Sallust but moved here in 1788.

Colonna dell'Immacolata

The column of the Immaculate Conception stands in the south eastern part of the Piazza Spagna and was erected in 1857 having been found underneath a monastery in 1777. The Pope visits the column each year on the 12th December. A statue of the Virgin Mary now stands on its top. The prophets Isaiah and Ezekiel are positioned at its base as well as the statues of Moses and David.

Fontana della Barcaccia

The Fountain of the old boat is a Baroque fountain that stands in the Piazza di Spagna just below the Spanish Steps. It was designed by Pietro Bernini and his son. It was built in the shape of a half-sunken boat with the water overflowing its bows. The design was inspired by the small boat that was left stranded after the Tiber flooded in 1598.

From the Barcaccia Fountain walk north on the Piazza di Spagna, turn left, then right in order to stay on Piazza di Spagna and continue onto Via del Babuino. After about 550 metres make a right turn into the Piazza del Popolo.

Piazza del Popolo

The People's Square is an oval shaped square that has been located in the northern part of the city since Roman times. There are three churches bordering the square, two fountains and an impressive ancient obelisk from Heliopolis in Egypt.

The Italian sculptor Giovanni Ceccarini embellished the walls that surround the square with statues of sphinxes and a flight of curving steps and ramps connects the square to the park on the Pincio hill above.

Porta del Popolo

The People's Gate is also known as the Porta Flaminia and stands on the north side of the square leading to the Via Flaminia which was built in 220 BC. The Via Flaminia was one of the most important roads leading to Rome, connecting the city with the Adriatic Coast.

The Porta del Popolo was a gate of the Aurelian Walls in Rome through which many visitors passed into Rome and was commissioned in 1562 by Pope Pius IV to impress the many pilgrims who travelled along the Via Flaminia.

Fontana del Nettuno

The Neptune Fountain stands at the western end of the Piazza del Popolo and was built in 1822 by Giovanni Ceccarini. Neptune holds his trident and stands between two Tritons.

Fontana della dea di Roma

The Fountain of the Goddess of Rome built in 1823 is also attributed to Giovanni Ceccarini. The group of carvings relate to the legends of the city of Rome.

The central figure of the carvings, armed with a lance and helmet is the goddess of Rome. On her right are the statues of Tiberio and Aniente who represent the Tiber and Aniene rivers. On her left there is the wolf feeding Romulus and Remus. The limestone basin that collects the water is shaped like a large shell.

The Piazza del Popolo with the Flaminio Obelisk and Twin Churches

Flaminio Obelisk

The Flaminio Obelisk is 24 metres high and now stands in the centre of the Piazza del Popolo. It is one of thirteen ancient obelisks found in Rome and was originally erected in the Circus Maximus after being brought back from the Sun Temple in Heliopolis to celebrate the defeat of Egypt on the orders of the Roman Emperor Augustus. Three of its sides were decorated by Seti I and the other by his son Ramses II.

When Giuseppe Valier redesigned the Piazza del Popolo in 1815 by adding walls decorated by the sculptor Giovanni Ceccarini the Obelisk was erected in the centre. At the base of the obelisk four Egyptian style lion fountains stand on a stepped plinth with the water spouting from their mouths, in the shape of arcs, falling into a large pool below each of the lions.

Iglesias de Santa Maria dei Miracoli and Santa Maria in Montesanto

The two churches of Saint Mary of the Miracles and Saint Mary of the Holy Mountain stand at the southern end of the square facing the northern gate of the Aurelian Walls.

They are often called the *twin churches* and thought to be symmetrical because they are so similar but they are in fact not identical. The churches were commissioned by Pope Alexander VII in 1658, designed by Carlo Rainaldi and financed by Cardinal Girolamo Gastaldi.

Santa Maria in Montesanto is the smaller church and stands on the left. It has an oval dome while that of the larger church, Santa Maria dei Miracoli, has a round dome.

Iglesia de Santa Maria del Popolo

The church of Saint Mary of the People is the third church in the square and stands to the north of the square near the Porta del Popolo. It was built on the site of an eleventh century chapel in 1477.

It has a spectacular Renaissance facade, a bell tower and octagonal cupola. The Chigi chapel was designed and decorated by Raphael and contains some beautiful Renaissance and Baroque art. The Della Rovere chapel has some splendid frescos including that of the Madonna and Child above the altar and the Assumption of the Virgin Mary. The church also has many other magnificent works of art that include two famous paintings by Carvaggion and the oldest stained glass windows in Rome.

The Second Tour

Today's walking tour begins at the Vatican and ends at Piazza Cavour. The nearest Metro station to the Vatican is Ottaviano which is on Line A while the nearest to the Piazza Cavour is Lepanto which is also on line A.

Main Sights

- The Vatican
- Vatican Museums
- Sistine Chapel
- Saint Peter's Square
- Saint Peter's Basilica
- Ponte Sant'Angelo
- Castel Sant'Angelo
- Palazzo di Giustizia
- Piazza Cavour

From Ottaviano Metro station walk west on the Viale Giulio Cesare for 10 metres before turning left onto Via Ottaviano. About 100 metres along this road turn right onto Via degli Scipioni and after 210 metres turn left onto Via Leone IV. After 40 metres turn right onto Viale Vaticano and the entrance to the Vatican will be on the left.

The Vatican

In order to visit the Vatican and avoid long queues it is best to book the Vatican tickets online from the official Vatican website: http://mv.vatican.va/3_EN/pages/MV_Home.html

Tickets can be bought at the ticket office between 9 a.m. and 4 p.m. on the day of your visit but be prepared to queue, sometimes for hours.

Pope Julius II began collecting works of art in 1506 but it was Pope Clement XIV and Pope Pius VI who were responsible for founding the Vatican Museums in the eighteenth century and the Pio-Clementine Museum is named after them. They were two of the first people to share works of art with the public. Today there are thirteen museums housed in the Belvedere and Apostolic palaces.

The Vatican complex served as the principal home of the popes and was built between the twelfth and nineteenth centuries. Two other buildings were joined to the palaces by Bramante in the sixteenth century to enclose a large courtyard known as the *Cortile del Belvedere* and later another wing was added to divide this courtyard in two and create a second courtyard known as the Pine Cone courtyard or *Cortile della Pigna.*

This courtyard takes its name from the spectacular bronze pine cone that is almost 4 metres high. It originally stood near the Pantheon in Rome and was an ancient fountain. The two bronze peacocks that stand on each side of the cone are replicas of ancient sculptures found in the Mausoleum of Hadrian.

In the middle of this courtyard there is also a modern bronze sculpture of two concentric spheres that was created by Arnaldo Pomodoro. It is known as *Sphere within a sphere.*

The Vatican Courtyard and the Pine Cone sculpture

Pinacoteca Vaticana

The Vatican Picture Gallery was established by Pius VI in the late eighteenth century but not opened until 1932. Many famous paintings from the Middle Ages until present day are housed in its sixteen halls.

One of the highlights includes the *Stefaneschi triptych* created by Giotto for the old church of St Peter about 1300. There are also the tapestries of the *Acts of the Apostles* created by Pieter van Aelst; the *Madonna* by Titian for the church Of San Nicolo in Venice; the *Stoning of Stephen* by Giogrio Vasari and the unfinished *St Jerome* by Leonardo da Vinci.

Museo Pio-Clementino

The Pio-Clementine Museum, named after the founders of the Vatican Museums, houses an extensive collection of ancient sculptures, enormous statues, busts and portraits that include many famous people, emperors, gods and heroes.

The marble copy of the famous bronze statue by Lysippos can be found here. The statue *Apoxyomenos* is known as the Scraper and depicts an athlete wiping the sweat from his body.

The *Apollo of Belvedere* which is a statue of Apollo described as aesthetically perfect can be found in the Cortile Ottagonale along with the famous sculpture group the *Laocoön*. The group created by three sculptors from Rhodes is praised for the dignified way it depicts agony.

In the Salle de Muse is the *Belvedere Torso* that portrays a powerful man's body on a rock which is said to have inspired Michelangelo with some of his paintings on the Sistine Chapel ceiling.

Other impressive works include the *Candelabri Barberini,* the *Aphrodite of Knidos,* the *Sleeping Ariadne* and the spectacular Roman mosaic in the Sala Rotonda which is a room modelled like the Pantheon.

Museo Gregoriano Eglizio

The Egyptian Museum is divided into nine rooms and has many Egyptian artefacts and monuments from Rome and the Villa Adriana. It includes the *Grassi Collection,* the famous *Book of the Dead* and animal mummies. Two rooms also have artefacts from Syria Palestine which was an ancient Roman province and also Mesopotamia.

Museo Gregoriano Etrusco

In 1837 Pope Gregory XVI founded the Estruscan Museum which holds the second most important Estruscan collection in Rome with bronzes, vases, sarcophagi and other archaeological finds from southern Etruria, Hellenistic Italian vases, Roman artefacts and the *Guglielmi Collection*.

The museum holds Iron Age objects dating back to the ninth century BC and the fifth century hollow bronze sculpture known as the *Mars of Todi*. There is a tall jug depicting Achilles and Ajax playing with dice and objects found in the *Regolini-Galassi* tomb at Cerveteri.

Museo Gregoriano Profano

The Gregorian Museum of Pagan Antiquities contains the collection once held in the Lateran Museum. It chronicles classical art from Ancient Greece up to the Imperial Roman era. Most artefacts come from discoveries made in the Papal States.

There are a number of funerary monuments and steles with sarcophagi, reliefs and statues as well as fragments from the Parthenon in Athens and mosaics of athletes from the Baths of Caracalla that were constructed in 212 AD. A copy of the original bronze *Athena and Marsyas* by the Greek sculptor Myron can also be seen here.

Museo Chiaramonti

The Chiaramonti Museum was founded by Pope Pius VII, a member of the Chiaramonti family and contains Greek and Roman works of art. In the extended new wing a superb Roman mosaic floor can be seen together with the sculpture of the Roman Emperor Augustus known as the *Augustus di Prima Porta*. The *Doryphoros,* known as the Spearman is regarded as a perfect example of a Greek statue. One highlight not to be missed is the statue of the Nile God Hapi that came from the Temple of Isis near the Pantheon.

Museo Pio Cristiano

The Pio Christian Museum has exhibits from early Christian times including sarcophagi, sculptures, inscriptions and mosaics. The most famous is the third century statue of the Good Shepherd.

Ethnoligical Museo Missionario

The Ethnological Missionary Museum was originally founded by Pope Pius XI in 1926 and relocated in the Vatican in 1973. It contains objects from Africa, America, Oceania and Asia.

Biblioteca Apostolica Vaticana

The Vatican Library is a research library thought to be founded by Pope Nicholas V in 1450 and officially established in 1475 by Pope Sixtus IV. It contains a huge number of books and incunabula from the Middle Ages as well as printed works up to the present day.

Cappella Sistina

The Sistine Chapel was built as a private chapel for Pope Sixtus IV between 1473 and 1481 by Giovannino de Dolci. In 1508 Pope Julius II commissioned Michelangelo to paint it. It took him four years and he created the magnificent frescoed ceiling as well as the fresco behind the altar known as *The last Judgement.*

The ceiling is divided into nine central sections that illustrate stories from the bible starting with the *Creation of Light* and ending with the *Drunkenness of Noah.* In the centre of the ceiling can be seen the famous image of the Finger of God breathing life into Adam.

The walls on the sides of the room were painted by well known Roman painters at the end of the fifteenth century under the guidance of Pinturicchio. These portray events that happened in the lives of Moses and Jesus.

On leaving the Vatican Museums walk east along Viale Vaticano. After 200 metres turn right onto Via Leone IV and continue onto Viale dei Bastioni di Michelangelo and Piazza del Risorgimento. Turn right onto Via di Porta Angelica which after 300 metres becomes Largo del Colonnato. Saint Peter's Square and basilica will be on the right.

Saint Peter's Square

Pope Alexander VII commissioned Bernini to create the great elliptical Saint Peter's Square in front of Saint Peter's basilica in 1656. It took eleven years to build.

The two semi-circular colonnades which border the square are said to symbolise the arms of the church welcoming the world. There are 140 statues created by Bernini and his students that stand on the top of the colonnades. They include religious figures such as saints, popes, martyrs and evangelists.

A 25 metre obelisk that was brought to Rome from Heliopolis in Egypt now stands in the centre of the square. It was originally installed in the Circus of Caligula but with a tremendous effort moved to the square in 1585 at the request of Pope Sixtus V.

The fountain by Carlo Maderno was installed in the square in 1613 but Bernini decided to install an identical copy by Carlo Fontana to retain the symmetry of the square in 1677.

Basilica di San Pietro

Saint Peter's Renaissance cathedral is one of the largest churches in the world and is visited by pilgrims and tourists from many countries. It stands to the west of the River Tiber on the Vatican Hill on the site where Saint Peter, now considered to have been the first pope, died as a martyr and was buried in 64 AD.

Emperor Constantine, who was the first Christian Emperor of Rome, commissioned the first basilica to be built in the fourth century on the site believed to be the grave of Saint Peter. By the middle of the fifteenth century the basilica was in decay and Pope Nicholas V organised some restoration work.

Having appointed Donato Bramante as the chief architect in 1506 Pope Julius II laid the first stone and the church was reconstructed. Many famous architects and builders were involved over the years when it was being built. In 1547

Michelangelo became the chief architect and formulated the idea for the impressive dome.

The church was extended as a Latin cross plan by Carlo Maderno who also completed the main facade in 1614. Pope Urban VIII consecrated the basilica in 1626.

Make sure you wear appropriate clothes for visiting the basilica.

Exterior Facade

The enormous facade of the cathedral is 115 metres long and 45.5 metres high; built from travertine stone. The extensive length is due to Pope Paul V wanting the cathedral to be connected to the Vatican Palace. Maderno used enormous columns, pillars, balconies, windows and entrances to create the facade. Statues, nearly six metres tall of Christ, John the Baptist and the apostles, except for Saint Peter, stand along it.

Two towers join each side of the front facade but were never extended above it because the ground was not stable enough to bear the weight of anything higher. At the top of each tower are huge clocks supported by carvings of angels and decorated with the papal crest and other ornaments. Below the clocks are the church bells, the oldest of which date from 1288.

Saint Peter's Basilica front façade

Portico

The entrance hall stretches across the whole building and was mainly designed by Maderno. On the left stands the equestrian statue of Charlemagne created by Agostino Cornacchini while on the right is the equestrian statue of Emperor Constantine by Bernini.

The central bronze door created by Antonio Averulino originally stood in the old church of Saint Peter and is known as the *Filarete door*. The bronze door on the right, known as the *Porta Santa* is a holy door which is only opened once every 25 years. It was built by Vico Consorti. The door on the far left into the basilica is known as the *Door of Death* because it was traditionally used as the exit for funeral processions.

Interior

The spectacular interior with its gigantic proportions and opulence contains numerous items to view and should not be missed. There are many chapels, altars and tombs as well as many rich Renaissance monuments, ornaments and works of art.

In the nave, just inside the central doors there is a round disc of red porphyry stone, taken from the old basilica, which marks the spot where Charlemagne and other Roman emperors knelt for their coronation.

The statues placed on the side pillars are of saints who founded different religious orders. In the north-west corner of the nave is the bronze statue of *Saint Peter Enthroned* by Alnolfo di Cambio.

In the chapel on the right aisle is the unique *Pietà* sculpture by Michelangelo that depicts the Virgin Mary cradling Jesus after the crucifixion. On the side pillar is a memorial plaque to Queen Christina of Sweden who renounced her throne to convert to Catholicism. The *Chapel of the Blessed Sacrament*, built by Bernini and Borromini, contains a gilded bronze tabernacle and the oil painting by Pietro da Cortona.

The altars of Saint Erasmus, Saint Processo and Saint Martiano as well as Saint Wenceslas are found in the right transept. The glass case beneath the *Altar of Saint Jerome* contains the body of Pope John XXIII who was beatified in 2000.

The papal altar, designed by Bernini, stands in the centre of the basilica over the grave of Saint Peter directly under the dome. Above it is the 26 metre high bronze *baldacchin*o that is made from 927 tons of bronze taken from the roof of the Pantheon. It is decorated with detailed motifs including bees and laurel leaves that were the heraldic emblems of the Barberini family as well as the Holy Spirit inside a radiant sun.

In front of the altar is the burial crypt known as the *confessio* which is surrounded by a balustrade with 95 gilded oil lamps where the eternal flame burns.

The four piers that support the great dome each have an enormous statue of a saint representing the basilica's four main relics. These are the cross held by Saint Helena, the spear of Saint Longinus, the head of Saint Andrew and the veil of Saint Veronica.

The left aisle and transept contain the *Altare della Monna della Colonna* which is the Altar of the Lady of the Column found inside the Chapel of the Column. Under the altar is the fourth century sarcophagus that holds the remains of Popes Leo II, Leo III and Leo IV. The altar of Saint Leo the Great is also within this chapel.

The Altar of Saint Gregory the Great is found to the east of the left transept in the Clementine Chapel with a mosaic by Sacchi depicting the miracle in which Saint Gregory causes blood to flow from a cloth. The altar of the last pope to be canonized, Pope Saint Pius X, is found in the *Presentation Chapel.*

The main focus for pilgrims and many tourists is the tomb of Saint Peter who was the very first pope. This can be found in the crypt underneath the church which also contains the tombs of many other popes as well as fragments of architecture from earlier churches.

The spectacular dome of Saint Peter's created by Michelangelo can be reached from an entrance near to the exit from the crypt. The gallery around the cupola of the dome is accessed by steps or by the elevator. From here inscriptions and the top of the baldacchino can be seen. Step out on the east side to see Saint Peter's Square and the Vatican City.

Climb even higher by taking the long, narrow spiral staircase to the roof to reach the viewing platform at the base of the dome's lantern which provides an excellent view of Rome.

If you feel you want to return to your hotel at this time the nearest metro station Ottaviano is a 10 minute walk away. To reach it walk north on Largo del Colonnato then turn slightly right onto Via di Porta Angelica then onto Via Ottaviano. Turn right onto Viale Giulio Cesare and the metro will be on the right. If you can manage it complete the tour and have your evening meal in or near Piazza Cavour.

To continue the tour leave Saint Peter's square and walk east along Piazza Papa Pio XII for about 50 metres then continue onto Via della Conicilizione, Lungotevere Vaticano and Lungotevere Castello. Turn right onto Ponte Sant'Angelo.

Ponte Sant'Angelo

The bridge of the Holy Angel across the Tiber River was originally constructed in 136 AD on the orders of Emperor Hadrian so that his mausoleum could be connected with the city of Rome and was originally known as *Pons Aelius* which means Hadrian's Bridge.

It then became known as Saint Peter's bridge when Saint Peter's basilica was built and the pilgrims passed over it on their way to Saint Peter's. According to legend in 590 AD the Archangel Michael was seen on the top of the mausoleum indicating the end of the plague that had gripped the city.

The bridge then became known as the *Ponte Sant'Angelo,* the bridge of the Holy Angel, and Hadrian's mausoleum was renamed the *Castel Sant'Angelo* or the Castle of the Holy Angel. The ten impressive angel sculptures that line the bridge were added in 1669 at the request of Pope Clement IX by Bernini and his students and tell the story of the suffering and crucifixion of Christ. Two of the statues, the Angel with the Superscription and the Angel with the Crown of Thorns, were kept by Pope Clement himself and can be seen today in *Sant'Andrea delle Fratte Iglesia* which is near the Spanish Steps.

Copies of these statues were created by Bernini's students and placed on the bridge instead. The statues of the apostles Peter and Paul stand at the southern end of the bridge in memory of the pilgrims who were killed here when a rider lost control of her horse in 1450.

Castel Sant'Angelo

The Castle of the Holy Angel was originally built by Emperor Hadrian on the bank of the River Tiber as a mausoleum for members of the Imperial family. It was fortified and used by previous popes who fled there in times of danger and there is still a secret corridor known as the *Passetto di Borgo* that connects it to the Vatican.

The bronze statue of the Archangel Michael sculptured by Pieter Verschaffelt stands on top of the fortress replacing the earlier marble one as a reminder of the archangel who was seen on the fortress in 590 AD.

Today the castle houses the *Museo Nationale de Castle Sant'Angelo* and has five floors. On the first is the impressive Roman winding ramp that was used for the funeral cortege.

In the past the castle was also used as a prison and one can still see the tiny cells where prisoners such as Cellini, Bruno and the fraudster Calgiostro were held on the second floor. The third floor has big courtyards and is military based with a display of ancient weapons.

Magnificent examples of art are found on the fourth floor known as the *Floor of the Popes* while the fifth floor has a terrace with some wonderful views of the city.

The Castel Sant'Angelo and Ponte Sant'Angelo over the River Tiber

After leaving the Castel Sant'Angelo walk north along the Ponte Sant'Angelo and turn right onto Lungotevere Castello. After 160 metres turn left onto Piazza Adriana. After 50 metres turn right to stay on Piazza Adriana and then after 60 metres left to continue on Piazza Adriana. When you meet Piazza dei Tribunali turn right.

Palazzo di Giustizia

The Palace of Justice is the seat of the Supreme Court and also houses the Judicial Public Library. It is a huge building with both Baroque and Renaissance features that fronts the Via dei Tribunali, the Piazza dei Tribunali, the Via Ulpiano and the Piazza Cavour.

The building, designed by Guglielmo Calderini, was built between 1888 and 1910 and is considered one of the most impressive new buildings since Rome was declared the capital of Italy. The facade overlooking the River Tiber has a huge bronze quadriga that was sculptured by Ettore Ximenes in 1926 while the facade overlooking the Piazza Cavour has the bronze coat of arms of the House of Savoy.

Continue walking east along Piazza dei Tribunali and after 100 metres turn left onto Via Ulpiano. Continue along this road until you reach Piazza Cavour.

The Palace of Justice seen from the Ponte Umberto I

Piazza Cavour

The Cavour square was built in 1876 and is dedicated to the important Italian statesmen Camillo Benso, the Count of Cavour. He was one of the important people who led an active part in the unification of Italy. His monument stands in the middle of the square and was designed by Galletti. It is a bronze statue that stands on a marble pedestal and granite platform.

Twin fountains stand at the edges of the central staircase of the Palace of Justice. The water in each fountain flows into an extended shell that overflows into the basin below. The gardens were created between 1895 and 1911 and provide a peaceful place to watch the world go by.

The buildings around the square date from the middle of the nineteenth century and include the *Teatro Adriano* and the *Chiesa Valdese*, a Waldenesian church.

If you need to use the metro to reach your hotel the nearest is Lepanto. From the Piazza Cavour walk northwest and join Via Cicerone. Continue along this road until it becomes Via Marcantonio Colonna. After about 350 metres turn right onto Viale Giulio Cesare and the Lepanto metro station will be on the left.

The Third Tour

Today's walking tour begins at Palatine Hill and ends at the Roman Forum. The nearest metro station to Palatine Hill and the Colosseum is Colosseo which is on Line B. If you exit the Roman Forum opposite the Colosseum the Colosseo metro station is about a three minute walk.

Main Sights:

- Palatine Hill
- House of Augustus and Imperial Palace
- Flavian Palace
- House of Livia
- Farnese Gardens
- Arch of Tito
- Colosseum
- Arch of Constantine
- Temple of Venus and Rome
- Roman Forum
- Arch of Septimius Severus

Leave the Colosseo Metro station and walk east on the Via Nicola Salvia. Just after Via Vittorino da Feltre on the left take the stairs on the right onto Piazza del Colosseo and turn right onto Piazza del Colosseo. Turn left onto Via dei Verbiti and you will see the Colosseum on your left.

Your entrance ticket to the Colosseum also includes entry to the Palatine Hill and the Roman Forum. If you have not bought your tickets online it might be advisable to visit the Palatine Hill first as there are rarely long queues from the entrance in Via di San Gregorio which is just a five minute walk from the Colosseum. The walk from Palatine Hill down to the Colosseum and Roman Forum is also easier this way.

To reach the entrance to Palatine Hill continue along Via dei Verbiti and then turn right onto Via di San Gregorio. After 200 metres turn right and take the stairs to the entrance to the Palatine Hill and Roman Forum.

Palatine Hill

The Palatine Hill stands above the Roman Forum and is one of the most ancient parts of the city. In mythology it is said to be where Romulus founded the city in 753 BC. Many important Roman families such as Marc Anthony had their homes on the hill and later many emperors built their imperial palaces here. Churches and convents were also built on the hill.

From the entrance on Via di San Gregorio walk west and climb the stairs. Turn right then a sharp left, and left again. Continue south-west for 4 metres then turn left for 12 metres to reach the Imperial Palace.

Domus Augustana and Imperial Palace

The Domus Augustana was once a magnificent palace used by the emperors of Rome. It was built by Emperor Domitian in 92 AD and today many of its walls as well as the remains of a fountain can be seen.

The palace overlooks the Circus Maximus where Tarquinius Priscus created a track between the Palatine and Aventine hills for chariot races to be held. The last race was held here in 549 AD.

The Imperial Palace on Palatine Hill overlooking the Circus Maximus

From the Imperial Palace walk north for 30 metres then make a slight right. The House of Augustus will be on the right.

Domus Augustea

Although later emperors lived in the magnificent palace built by Domitian the House of Augustus was the much more humble home and the first Roman Emperor Augustus lived there. The Palatine Museum is located here.

From the Domus Augustea walk southeast for 40 metres then turn left, left again then right. After 35 metres turn left and left again.

Domus Flavia

The Flavian Palace was part of the huge residential complex of the Roman Emperors and was completed in 92 AD by Titus Flavius Domitanus who is also known as Emperor Domitian. The palace had floors and walls that were decorated with coloured marble and was used for important state functions. It has the remains of impressive fountains in its courtyard.

From the Domus Flavia walk north-west and take the stairs then after 40 metres turn left and the House of Livia will be on the right.

House of Livia

The house of Livia was built in the first century and was the home of Emperor Augustus and his wife Livia. It is one of the best preserved houses on the Palatine hill. It is a two-storey house built around a central hall that contains detailed frescoes of mythology.

From the House of Livia walk south-east for 200 metres and Orti Farnesiani sul Palatino will be ahead.

Orti Farnesiani sul Palatino

The Farnese Gardens were created in 1550 as a summer residence for Cardinal Allesandro Farnese. The ruins of the Palace of Tiberius originally stood here but the garden was built on top of the ruins and so much has disappeared. It was one of the first botanical gardens in Europe.

As you climb the stairs to the gardens you pass an artificial grotto known as the *Nymphaeum* which is dedicated to the nymphs of the springs. Further up are the Farnese aviaries. From the top are superb views of Rome that include Saint Peter's basilica and the Victor Emanuele II monument.

Walk north-east and take the stairs then turn left towards Via Sacra then right and take the stairs. Turn right again onto Via Sacra.

Arco di Tito

The Arch of Titus was constructed in the first century by Titus's brother Emperor Domitian to honour the victories of Titus in the Jewish War. The 15 metre tall Roman arch is the oldest that survives. There are two panels with reliefs inside the arch known as the *Spoils of Jerusalem*. The arch was restored by Guiseppe Valier in 1821.

Walk east on the Via Sacra for about 200 metres then turn left onto Via dei Verbiti and right onto Piazza del Colosseo. The Colosseum is straight ahead.

Colosseo

The Colosseum is an oval amphitheatre that was constructed by the three emperors of the Flavian dynasty following the reign of Nero and is also referred to as the *Flavian Amphitheatre*. It takes its name from the colossal statue of Nero that originally stood here.

Started by the Emperor Vespasian in 72 AD the Colosseum is the largest amphitheatre in the world and considered to be a masterpiece of Roman architecture and engineering. It was completed in 80 AD under the guidance of Vespasian's son Titus who also added the fourth floor. To mark the inauguration of the building in this year Titus organised 100 days of games.

The immense building measures 188 metres by 156 metres and stands almost 50 metres high. It was clad in travertine marble and covered with a *velarium*, an enormous awning that protected the spectators from the sun, held in place by large poles on top of the Colosseum that were anchored to the ground by ropes.

The four storeys of the Colosseum could hold up to 73,000 spectators. Entertainment was free for everyone but the lower classes sat on the upper storey while important people sat on the lower storeys. Animals were housed in cages underground that were lifted using mechanical devices into the centre of the arena. The locker rooms and gladiator's training rooms can still be seen today.

The Colosseum

The arena was used for gladiatorial contests, executions, dramas, portrayals of past battles and other public spectacles. After these were discontinued the Colosseum began to fall into decay. Over the years earthquakes such as the one that destroyed the southern side in 847 AD and stone robbers have resulted in parts of the building falling into ruin but it is still a spectacular sight. The marble cladding and old stone blocks were used in other buildings around Rome including Saint Peter's Basilica and the Palazzo Farnese.

From the Colosseum walk south on Piazza del Colosseo then turn right and right again and you will see the Arch of Constantine.

Arco di Costantino

The Arch of Constantine which stands next to the Colosseum is the largest and most recent of the three arches of triumph built on the Roman Forum. The arch was built in 312 AD to commemorate Emperor Constantine's victory over Maxentius at the Milvian Bridge which brought peace to the empire.

The structure is 21 metres tall and 26 metres high and is built from a large central archway with a smaller one to each side. Many older monuments were used to decorate the structure such as the statues that stand on the top taken from the Forum of Trajan. Relief panels were created for Marcus Aurelius while other parts are from the era of Emperor Hadrian. Some scenes have little connection to Constantine's battles.

The Arch of Constantine viewed from the Colosseum

From the Arch of Constantine walk northwest on Via dei Verbiti and the Temple of Venus and Rome will be on the left.

Templum Veneris et Romae

The Temple of Venus and Rome was the largest temple in ancient Rome and was dedicated to the goddess Venus. It was designed by Emperor Hadrian and completed in 141 AD in the reign of Antonius Pius.

The temple was built on the remains of the Domus Aurea of Nero and so the huge statue of Nero had to be moved and was placed inside the Flavian amphitheatre. The temple was destroyed twice, once by a fire and later by an earthquake. After the earthquake Pope Leo IV ordered that a church be built over the ruins of the temple and named it the Santa Maria Nova. The church was renamed the Santa Francesca Romana after it was again rebuilt in 1612 .

There is an exit from the Roman Forum opposite the Colosseum but the main entrance to the Roman Forum is from Via di San Pietro in Carcere off the Via Dei Fori Imperiali.

From the Temple of Venus and Rome walk north on Piazza del Colosseo then turn left onto Via Dei Fori Imperiali and walk for about 650 metres. Turn left onto Via di San Pietro in Carcere. After 200 metres take a sharp left and take the stairs to the Roman Forum.

The Roman Forum with the Altar of the Fatherland in the background

Forum Romanum

The Roman Forum stood on drained marshland and was the political centre for Rome, its market place and its social centre. It was the place where the senate held their meetings and elections were held.

The oldest monuments date back to the sixth century but many of the buildings are from different eras as the abandoned forum became covered by a layer of mud and some temples were transformed into churches. Today among the ruins are fallen columns, walls, basilicas and temples. It should not be confused with the Imperial Forums that were built at a later date.

Arco di Settimio Severo

The Arch of Septimius Severus was built and dedicated in 203 AD to commemorate the victories of Septimius Severus over the Parthians and is one of the finest preserved monuments in the forum.

The white marble arch is 23 metres high and 25 metres wide. It has three arched passageways. The road that runs through the central one replaced a flight of stairs in the fourth century.

Curia Julia

The original Curia where the senate sat burned down four times. The present building was built in the reign of Diocletian in 283 AD and turned into a church during the seventh century.

The Rostra and Tetrachy

The Rostra was the speaker's platform from where the orators spoke to the people. The Tetrachy was a five pillared monument built behind the Rostra to celebrate the twentieth year of the reign of Diocletian.

Temple of Saturn

The Temple of Saturn was built in the fourth century to honour the god Saturn and was where the original festival of Saturnalia was celebrated. It has eight majestic columns and during the Republic it housed the public treasury.

Next to the Temple of Saturn is a fragment of the *Milliarium Aaureum*, the Golden Milestone. This marked the beginning and end of all Roman roads and displayed the distance between Rome and its provinces.

Phocus Column

The Corinthian Phocus Column is 14 metres high and is the newest building in ancient Rome. It was built to honour the Byzantine Emperor Phocus on his visit to Rome.

The Temple of Saturn

Temple of Caesar

The Temple of Caesar was built by Augustus in 29 BC to honour Julius Caesar on the spot where he was cremated after being murdered. In front of the temple is the Rostra Julia which was the speaker's platform that was decorated with the prows of conquered ships.

Temple of Vesta

The Temple of Vesta is a circular structure that dates back to the fourth century BC and though small was an important temple because it was dedicated to Vesta the goddess of the hearth who protected the family and state.

Near to the Temple of Vesta is the House of the Vestal Virgins that was home for girls aged six and over who were specially chosen. The Vestal Virgins guarded the eternal flame burning in the temple which was a symbol of the eternal life of Rome.

Temple of Antoninus and Faustina

The Temple of Antoninus and Faustine was built by Antoninus Pius in 141 AD to honour his wife Faustina. It is still in an excellent condition today, probably because in the seventh century it was converted to the church of San Lorenzo in Miranda which was rebuilt in 1601.

Temple of Castor and Pollux

The Temple of Castor and Pollux that stands in the middle of the Forum was built in 500 AD to celebrate the Roman victory at the Battle of Lake Regillus. The temple was built on the spot that legend decrees the twins Castor and Pollux brought back news of the victory. Today only three pillars remain.

Basilica Aemilia

The Basilica Aemilia was erected in 179 BC and is the oldest church in the forum. It was built by Marcus Aemilius Lepidus and Marcus Fulvius Nobilior. It was originally considered one of the most beautiful buildings in Rome and was used as a meeting place for business. In 22 AD a great marble hall was created and money exchanges, banks and shops were housed here.

Basilica Julia

The construction of the once ornate Basilica Julia was begun in 54 BC with the intention of providing a public building that could be used for meetings and other official business. The civil law courts were located inside as well as shops, government offices and banks.

To reach the Colosseo Metro station exit the Roman Forum opposite the Colosseum and follow Via dei Verbiti until it meets Piazza del Colosseo. Turn right onto Piazza del Colosseo and take the steps to Via Nicola Salvi. The metro station is on the left.

The Fourth Tour

Today's tour begins at the Piazza Quirinal and ends at the Domus Aurea. Instructions are given from the nearest metro stations at the beginning and end of the tour which are Barberini and Colosseo.

Main Sights:

- Piazza Quirinal
- Quirinal Palace
- Fontana di Monte Cavallo
- Piazza Venezia
- Palazzo Venezia
- Vittorio Emanuel II monument
- Imperial Forums
- Trajan's Forum
- Trajan's Column and Market
- Basilica di San Pietro in Vincoli
- Domus Aurea

From Barberini metro station walk south west on the Piazza Barberini for 60 metres then turn left onto Via della Quattro Fontane. After 270 metres turn right onto Via del Quirinale and turn right into Piazza Quirinale.

Piazza Quirinale

The Quirinale Square is located on top of the Quirinale Hill which is the highest of the Seven Hills of Rome. Besides the beautiful buildings and other structures one side of the square has a wonderful view over the city of Rome towards Saint Peter's Basilica.

If you walk down the steps towards the Salita di Montecavallo you will see seven statues carved into the walls that were installed in 1866.

Palazzo del Quirinale

The Quirinale Palace that stands to the north of the square is the ninth largest palace in the world and since the Unification of Italy in 1870 has been home to its president. The early Romans built temples on this hill in honour of different gods but the current palace was built by Pope Gregory XIII in 1583 as his summer residence.

Many popes played a part in building its various parts but the heraldic symbols of Pope Paul V can be found everywhere. Pope Urban VIII fortified the palace in 1626 by building high walls on its western side and a round tower near its entrance. However, they were not strong enough to prevent the French from capturing the pope in later centuries.

Domenico Fontana decorated the facade and the Great Chapel was created by Carlo Maderno. The palace houses numerous collections of art and inside the monumental staircase hall there is a superb fresco by Melozzo da Forlì. The gardens are also impressive. If you want to explore inside the palace then book your tickets online before arriving in Rome.

Palazzo Pallavicini-Rospigliosi

The Palace of Pallavicini-Rospigliosi was built by Cardinal Scipione Borghese as a summer residence for his uncle. The palace was built over the ruins of the Baths of Constantine which still form part of the basement of the building. It is owned by the Pallavicini family who still live in part of it and retain their original art gallery. The painting by Guido Reni is the only one that can be viewed by the public and that is only on the first day of the month.

Palazzo della Consulta

The Palace of the Consulate is a Baroque palace that was commissioned by Pope Clement XII and the papal court. It was built by Ferdinando Fuga in 1734 and is now the home of the Italian Constitutional Court.

Scuderie del Quirinale

The Quirinale Stables, also known as the Papal Stables, were designed by Ferdinando Fuga and built between 1722 and 1732. They were recently restored by Gae Aulent and now house art exhibitions.

Quirinale Obelisk

The obelisk that stands in the centre of the piazza was originally in the Mausoleum of Augustus. Pope Pius VII arranged for it to be erected in the Quirinale Square in 1786.

Fontana di Monte Cavallo

The Quirinale obelisk now forms part of the Quirinale fountain that is also known as the Dioscuri Fountain. On each side stand the great sculptures of Castor and Pollux as horse tamers.

These statues were originally located at the entrance to the Baths of Constantine but were placed in the piazza in 1588 by Pope Sixtus V and today are Roman copies of the Greek originals. The granite basin for the fountain was designed by Rafael Stern who used an ancient Roman shell from the Roman Forum. It was placed here in 1818.

The Quirinal Obelisk and Dioscuri Fountain in Quirinal Square

From the Piazza Quirinale walk east and turn right onto Via XXIV Maggion. At the roundabout take the second exit onto Via IV Novembre. You will see the Torre della Milizie on your left. Continue onto Via Magnanapoli and take the stairs. Continue onto Piazza Foro Traiano where you will see part of the Imperial Forums on your left and the churches of Santissimo Nome di Maria and Santa Maria di Loreto on your right.

Chiesa Santissimo Nome di Maria al Foro Traiano

The Church of the Most Holy Name of Mary can be found at the Trajan Forum. It is a Roman Catholic Church built in the eighteenth century although the first church on the site was that of Saint Bernard in 1418.

The interior with its polychrome marbles is worth a quick visit. It has a ceiling fresco of *Saint Bernard in Glory* by Avanzino Nucci and an image of the Virgin and Child painted on wood at the main altar.

Chiesa Santa Maria di Loreto

The Church of Saint Mary of Loreto is also next to the Trajan Forum. It was built in the sixteenth century by Antonio da Sangallo the Younger with the dome and the lantern being completed 75 years later by Jacopo del Duca.

The interior has a number of statues including those by Andrea Sansovino and Stefano Maderno as well as the famous early Baroque statue of Santa Susanna by Francois Duquesnoy. The mosaic chapel is also worth a look.

Turn left onto Piazza della Monna di Loreto and right to stay on this road before turning left onto the Piazza Venezia.

Piazza Venezia

The busy Venetian Square is located where several routes intersect and takes its name from the Venetian Palace that was built here. Although busy traffic wise it is the centre of many interesting attractions.

Palazzo Venezia

The Venetian Palace is one of the oldest civil Renaissance buildings in Rome and was built between 1455 and 1464 by Cardinal Pietro Barbo who later became Pope Paul II. The

Venetian Pope would watch North African horses racing down the Via del Corso from this palace.

Pope Pius IV gave the building to Venice as their embassy but in 1916 the Italian Government took charge of it. Mussolini addressed the public from the palace's balcony and used the building as his headquarters. Today it houses the Palazzo Venezia National Museum.

Monumento Nazionale a Vittorio Emanuele II

The immense marble Victor Emanuele Monument was built in honour of Victor Emmanuel who was the first king of a unified Italy. It stands between the Piazza Venezia and the Capitoline Hill. It is also known as the *Altar of the Fatherland*.

Giuseppe Sacconi designed the monument in 1885 but it was not completed until 1925. It has beautiful stairways and Corinthian columns. Under the statue of the goddess Roma is the Tomb of the Unknown Warrior where the eternal flame burns.

The Victor Emanuele Monument and Tomb of the Unknown Warrior

There are a number of magnificent statues that include an equestrian sculpture of Victor Emanuel as well as two statues of the goddess Victoria riding on quadrigas. The basement holds a museum dedicated to the history of the unification of Italy and it is possible to take the panoramic lift up to the roof from where you can see all over Rome.

Palazzo delle Assicurazioni Generali

The General Insurance Company building stands directly opposite the Palazzo Venezia. It was built between 1906 and 1911 by the architect Pazzi with many of its elements direct replicas of the Venetian Palace.

Palazzo Bonaparte

The Bonaparte Palace stands at the northern end of Piazza Venezia and was built in 1660 by Giovanni Antonio De Rossi for the Marquis Giuseppe Benedetto. It is an elegant building with three storeys and gabled windows as well as a covered balcony.

After Napoleon was exiled his mother Letizia was granted asylum in Rome and she lived in this palace until she died in 1936. It is now known as the Palazzo Misciatelli.

On leaving the Piazza Venezia return to the Piazza Forno Triaiano and explore the Imperial Forums including Trajan's Column, Trajan's Forum, and Trajan's market.

The Imperial Forums

The Imperial Forums are newer than the Roman Forums and were built between 46 BC and 113 AD. The Imperial Forums were originally self-contained areas that were intended for pedestrians. They were the nucleus of city life where religious, administrative, educational and commercial activities took place. Many emperors such as Augustus and Trajan also added their forums in this area. Julius Caesar was the first emperor to build here.

The Imperial Forums are today divided by the Via dei Fori Imperiali because in the early twentieth century Mussolini ordered the building of this road right across the site. It is said he wanted to be able to see the Colosseum from his house in the Piazza Venezia.

Foro di Cesare

The Forum of Caesar was the first of the Imperial Forums and was built after Caesar convinced Cicero and Oppius to persuade the original owners to sell their land. It was completed by Augustus in 29 BC. The large plaza was surrounded by colonnades and had a temple dedicated to Venus in the northwest as Caesar believed himself to be a direct descendent of this god. The forum was later rebuilt by Trajan in 113 AD.

Foro di Augusto

The Forum of Augustus was the second Imperial Forum to be built and was located adjacent to Caesar's forum. It was built both as a house and temple to honour the god Mars in order to avenge the assassination of Julius Caesar. The senate sat here when discussing matters of war and it is the place from where the military generals set off for their battles.

The open plaza was lined with colonnades and statues of famous leaders were placed in the niches. The statue of Augustus that stood here was 14 metres tall.

Foro Traiano

Trajan's forum was the last Imperial Forum to be built and certainly the grandest. It was commissioned by Trajan and designed by the architect Apollodorus of Damascus to celebrate Trajan's victories over the Dacians in the battles between 101 and 106 AD. It was completed in 113 AD after the soil had been excavated to a depth of 42 metres.

The forum had a great plaza with a large bronze equestrian statue of Trajan. It was lined on its sides by colonnades and the Basilica Ulpia stood at the northern end with Trajan's column standing behind. There were also two libraries and the large Temple of Divius Trainus.

Trajan's Column

With a height of 42 metres including its base Trajan's column towers over the forum. It was designed to match the height of the hill that originally stood on the site and commemorates Trajan's victories depicted by the two thousand carved figures that spiral around it.

Trajan's Forum

A six metre statue of the emperor now stands at the top of the column replacing the original statue of an eagle. The ashes of Trajan and his wife Plotina are held within the base of the column.

A flat replica of the column can be seen in the forum so that the story it tells can be enjoyed by everyone. It is more than 180 metres long and tells the story of his battles from when the soldiers prepared for war until the Dacians were defeated.

Trajan's Market

The semi-circular covered complex of Trajan's market was built between 107 AD and 110 AD by the architect Apollodorus of Damascus and represents the ancient equivalent of a modern shopping centre with around 150 shops and offices.

The market is set into the side of the Quirinal Hill and is bordered by a row of columns. It is still possible to walk along the Via Biberatica which was the main shopping street.

Having explored the Piazza Forro Traiano walk south-east and take the Via Alessandrina. After 250 metres turn left onto Via dei Fori Imperiali and almost immediately left onto Largo Corro Ricci. Continue onto Via Cavour for 350 metres before turning right at Salita dei Borgia and taking the stairs. Turn left onto Via S Francesco di Paola and take the stairs again. The Basilica di San Pietro in Vincoli will be on the left.

Basilica di San Pietro in Vincoli

The Church of Saint Peter in Chains is a small Roman Catholic church named after the chains that held Saint Peter when he was imprisoned. They can be seen at the confessio in front of the high altar.

People flock to the church not only to see the chains that supposedly held Saint Peter but also to see the tomb of Pope Julius II and marvel at the colossal Moses sculpture created by Michelangelo in 1505 which forms the centrepiece of the unfinished tomb.

On the ceiling there is also a magnificent painting by Giovanni Battista Parodi that depicts the Miracle of the Chains.

From the Basilica walk north on Piazza di San Pietro and then turn right onto Via delle Sette Sale. After 220 metres turn right onto Via Luigi Cremona where you will find the Domus Aurea.

Domus Aurea

After the great fire in Rome Nero had a new palace built that had walls covered with marble and vaults decorated with gold. It was designed by Severus and Celer then decorated by Fabullus the painter earning itself the name meaning Golden House.

When Nero died the rulers that followed tried to destroy all evidence of the palace covering it with soil. They built the large baths of Titus and Trajan on top and the Colosseum nearby. The treasures of the palace remained hidden until the Renaissance.

The palace has only recently opened to the public but it is now possible to book tickets online. Even if you do not visit the palace interior a walk around the Colle Oppio Park to see the ancient ruins that remain and also for the views of some of the most important monuments in Rome is worthwhile.

From the Domus Aurea walk south through the park and turn right and right again onto Viale del Monte Oppio. After 100 metres turn left onto Via delle Terme di Tito before turning right onto Via Nicola Salvi. Stay on this road until you meet the Colosseo metro station.

The Fifth Tour

Today's walking tour begins at the Piazza Venezia and ends at the Piazza della Minerva. Both of these areas are some distance from metro stations so it is preferable to either walk to and from your hotel or take a bus.

Main Sights:
- Piazza del Campidoglio
- Capitoline Museums and Palaces
- Teatro di Marcello
- Piazza Bocca della Verita and temples
- Chiesa di Santa Maria in Cosmedin
- Mouth of Truth
- Palazzo Spada
- Piazza Farnese and Palace
- Piazza di Campo dei Fiori
- Palazzo della Cancelleria
- Largo di Torre Argentina
- Chiesa del Santissimo Nome di Gesù
- Chiesa Santa Maria Sopra Minerva

From the Piazza Venezia walk north on the Via del Teatro di Marcello and after 10 metres turn right and take the stairs to the Basilica di Santa Maria in Aracoeli

Basilica di Santa Maria in Aracoeli

The Church of Saint Mary of the Altar of Heaven is one of the oldest churches in Rome and built on the ancient temple of Juno at the top of the Capitoline Hill. Emperor Augustus is said to have had a vision telling him about the arrival of the first born god so he built an altar on the top of the hill.

The main entrance to the church is reached by climbing 124 steep steps that are often referred to as *the Stairway to Heaven* because they lead to the *Altar of Heaven.*

An Italian politician, Cola di Rienzo, organised the building of the steps by Simeone Andreozzi to thank the Virgin Mary for the end of the plague in 1348.

Between the steps to the church and the Cordonata that leads up to Piazza del Campidoglio is a statue erected in his honour 523 years after he was killed by a mob that tore him to pieces.

The church has relics that belonged to Saint Helena, Constantine's mother. The San Bernardino Chapel has frescoes created by Bernardino Pinturicchio that describe the life of Saint Bernardine of Siena. To the right of the door is the tomb of Donatello and there are other works by notable artists such Michelangelo and paintings such as the tenth century *Madonna d'Aracoeli.*

The statue known as the *Santo Bambino* is a copy of the famous original stolen in 1994. It is a statue of the baby Jesus carved from olive wood that grew in the garden of Gethsemane. It was once believed that the statue could heal the terminally ill and even raise people from the dead.

The church has a beautiful sixteenth century ceiling decorated with nautical themes to commemorate the battle of Lepanto when the allied troops defeated the Turkish Fleet in 1571.

From the Basilica di Santa Maria in Aracoeli walk west and take the stairs down towards Via del Teatro di Marcello and turn left. After 110 metres take the stairs up to Capitol Square.

Piazza del Campidoglio

The *Cordonata staircase* is a sloping road broken into a series of wide steps that leads up to the Capitoline Square situated between the two peaks of the Capitoline Hill. The two lions that stand at the bottom are real Egyptian sculptures as well as the statues of Castor and Pollux at the top.

There are also statues of the Emperor Constantine and his son and the equestrian bronze gilded statue of Emperor Marcus Aurelius that stands in the middle of the square. The statue is a replica but the original one can be seen in the Capitoline Museums.

The Emperor Marcus Aurelius statue in the Piazza del Campidoglio

Many important buildings stood here and it was the home of the senate later becoming the political and religious centre of the ancient world.

When this beautiful Capitoline Square was redesigned by Michelangelo he adapted some of the existing buildings such as Palazzo Senatori and the facade of the Palazzo dei Conservatori. A new palace known as the Palazzo Nuovo was to be sited opposite the Palazzo dei Conservatori. Only the Palazzo Senatorio staircase was built before Michelangelo died. The project was completed as he had designed in the seventeenth century.

Palazzo Senatorio

The Palace of the Senators is the oldest building in the square and was where the Roman Senate met. It was originally a fortress that was rebuilt over the centuries. The statues that stand on either side of the grand double staircase were found in the ruins of the Baths of Constantine and represent the Rivers Nile and Tiber. There is also a statue of the goddess Minerva in the central recess that was modified to symbolise Roma.

Palazzo Nuovo

Opposite the Palazzo dei Conservatori is its mirror image known as the New Palace. It was completed by Carlo and Girolamo Rainaldi in 1654. It held an art collection that was made available to the public by Pope Clement XII in 1734 and today forms part of the Capitoline Museums.

Palazzo dei Conservatori

The Palace of the Conservators upon which the Palazzo Nuovo is modelled was built in 1563 and was the seat of the city magistrates. Like the Palazzo Nuovo this palace is now part of the Capitoline Museums.

Musei Capitolini

The Capitoline Museums housed in the Palazzo Nuovo and Palazzo dei Conservatori are connected by an underground tunnel. Although the present museums were designed by Michelangelo in 1536 they are in fact the oldest public museums in the world dating back to 1471 AD when Pope Sixtus IV donated artworks for public viewing.

Today the collection of classical sculpture is among the finest in Italy. Inside the Palazzo dei Conservatori are marble pieces from the gigantic statue of Emperor Constantine that stood on the Roman Forum. There are also tapestries, paintings and frescoes. Fresco scenes depicting the history of Rome can be seen in the *Hall of the Orazi e Curiazi.*

The famous statues of the *Spinario* and the *Lupa Capitolina* can also be found here as well as a bust of Hercules and the original equestrian statue of Marcus Aurelius. There is a picture gallery with paintings dating from the fourteenth to seventeenth century, coins, medals, jewellery and a porcelain collection.

The Palazzo Nuovo has intricate mosaics, busts, sarcophagi and statues together with famous sculptures such as the *Dying Gaul* that came from Caesar's gardens and the *Capitoline Venus.* The *Old Centaur* and the *Young Centaur,* two statues that came from the Villa of Hadrian, can be found in the Great Hall together with the beautiful *Dove's Mosaic.*

On leaving Capitol Square you can take the steps down or descend by the Via della Tre Pile. On reaching Via del Teatro di Marcello turn left and after 180 metres turn right onto Via Montanara for access to the Marcello Theatre.

Teatro di Marcello

The Theatre of Marcellus built in 13 BC to honour Marcellus by Emperor Augustus was the largest theatre in ancient Rome. It is one of the oldest examples of places where the ancient Romans were entertained.

When Julius Caesar defeated his rival Pompey it marked the end of the Roman Republic. Caesar planned a new theatre even though one built by Pompey already existed. He took over land and demolished the buildings that stood upon it including two temples. Caesar died soon after the building began and it was his successor Emperor Augustus who completed the project.

The impressive, semi-circular, open-air building completed in 11 BC was over 30 metres high. It had three tiers each with 41 arches and the top part was decorated with enormous marble theatre masks. The theatre could hold up to 20,000 spectators.

Today only the first two tiers of the theatre can be seen. During the twelfth century if was transformed into a fortress by the Fabii family and then the Savelli family who changed it into a fortified palace.

The Theatre of Marcellus

After visiting the theatre return to Via del Teatro di Marcello and after 100 metres bear left to stay on this road. Continue onto Via Luigi Petroselli until you meet the Piazza della Bocca dellar Verità.

Piazza Bocca della Verità

The Mouth of Truth Square is located in the ancient area of Rome near to Tiber Island that was known as the *Forum Boarium*. This was the cattle market of ancient Rome and the main port. The first gladiatorial contest was held here and it was a religious centre too. It was the place where death sentences were performed until 1668.

The square takes its name from the *Bocca della Verità*, the Mouth of Truth, which can be seen in the portico of the church of Santa Maria in Cosmedin. Besides the church there are also temples and a fountain.

Arco di Jano Quadrifrons

The huge marble Arch of Janus was built in the fourth century during the reign of Emperor Constantine I using materials from older Roman ruins. It is the only four gated arch to be preserved in Rome and was the meeting place for the cattle market merchants.

The god Janus was often depicted as having four faces which was probably the reason the arch was built with four *quadrifrons* or fronts. The four keystones of the arch portray Minerva, Ceres, Juno and Roma.

Tempio di Ercole Vincitore

The Temple of Hercules Victor is thought to be the oldest marble temple in Rome. The round temple encircled by a colonnade was commissioned by a local merchant and designed in the second century BC by the architect Hermodorus of Salamis. Inside the temple stood a statue of the god Hercules created by the sculptor Scopas. Today it is on display at the Capitoline museum.

Tempio di Portuno

The Temple of Portunus is a rectangular shaped temple dedicated to Portunus the god of ports and water crossings. The temple built from travertine and tufa was restored around 80 BC but dates back to the sixth century BC.

The temple rests on a high podium and is reached by a flight of steps. It was used as a church after the decline of the Roman Empire. The columns of the portico are free standing while the others are built into the walls.

Fontana dei Tritoni

The Fountain of the Tritons stands in the Piazza Bocca della Verità in front of the two ancient temples. It was designed by the architect Carlo Francesco Bizzaccheri and completed in 1715.

The fountain is a sculpture created by two tritons kneeling upon a group of rocks and holding an oyster shell upper basin on their shoulders. The pope's coat of arms sits between them. Water flows into a star shaped octagonal basin that was the heraldic symbol of the Albanis who were the pope's family.

Continue from Piazza della Bocca della Verità until you reach Santa Maria in Cosmedin and the Mouth of Truth.

Chiesa di Santa Maria in Cosmedin

The original small church that stood on this site dates back to the sixth century. When it was enlarged in the eighth century the Temple of Ceres and the Altar of Hercules were destroyed in order to extend it. The church was then named the Church of Saint Mary In Cosmedin.

The portico where the *Bocca della Verità* can be seen and the medieval bell tower which is the tallest in Rome were constructed in the twelfth century.

In this portico there is a monument to Cardinal Alphanus who oversaw the restoration of the church in the early twelfth century.

The marble door has eleventh century carvings by Giovanni di Venetia. The church has three naves and contains ancient Corinthian columns as well as a beautiful Cosmatesque floor. There are two marble pulpits and a Presbyterian throne with lions' heads.

The high altar contains the skull of Saint Valentine and in front of this altar is an eighth century mosaic. The ancient Gothic baldachin over the main altar is signed by Deodato di Cosma and dated to 1294.

The Mouth of Truth in Saint Mary in Cosmedin Church

Bocca della Verità

The Mouth of Truth is a giant marble disc that stands against the wall in the portico of the Church of Saint Mary in Cosmedin. The flat marble disc has a bearded face with an open mouth that probably represents the sea god Neptune.

The disc is believed to be an ancient drain cover although it could also have been part of a wall fountain. Legend has it that the mouth will close on the any hand put inside it if that person had previously lied. The Mouth of Truth featured in an American Movie made in 1953 known as *Summer Holiday*.

On leaving Santa Maria in Cosmedin walk across the Piazza towards the River Tiber and turn right onto Lungotevere Aventino. Continue onto Lungototevere dei Pierleoni and you will pass Tiber Island on your left. Walk onto until you reach Lungotevere dei Vallati and continue for 300 metres until you reach Ponte Sisto.

If you cross Ponte Sisto you will reach the area known as Trastevere where there are a number of restaurants and other sights to visit.

From Ponte Sisto turn right onto Via dei Pettinari then turn left onto Via Capo di Ferro and the Palazzo Spalda will be on the left.

Palazzo Spada

The Spada Palace was built in the sixteenth century by Giulio Mersi da Caravaggio for Cardinal Capodiferro with the elaborate stucco decoration by Giulio Mazzoni.

The palace passed to the Mignanelli family and then in 1632 to Cardinal Spada who asked Borromini to restore the palace. One notable feature is the perception of depth in the courtyards created by a coffered barrel vault giving the impression of a corridor 25 metres long that in reality has only a length of 10 metres.

The facade of the palace has the statues of eight famous Romans known as Augustus, Caesar, Marcellus, Numa Pompilius, Romulus, Maximus, Pompey and Trajan. Today the palace houses a small art gallery belonging to the Spada family which includes works by Andrea del Sarto, Guido Reni, Titian and Guercino.

From the Pallazo Spalda continue along Via Capo di Ferro and onto Vicolo dei Venti then turn right onto Piazza Farnese and after 17 metres left to stay on Piazza Farnese. The Palazzo Farnese will be on the left.

Piazza Farnese

The beautiful Farnese Square is located in the heart of medieval Rome. It has twin fountains designed by Rainaldi who used two baths of Egyptian granite brought from the Baths of Caracalla in the sixteenth century. They are fed by water from the Acqua Paola.

The upper part of the fountain has the emblems of the Farnese family and Cardinal Alessandro Farnese who became Pope Paul III. The small Swedish church of Saint Bridget also stands in the square.

Palazzo Farnese

The Renaissance Farnese Palace was originally designed in 1517 for the Farnese family by Antonio da Sangallo the Younger but when he died Michelangelo took charge. It was completed by Giacomo della Porta in 1589.

Like the fountains in the square much of the stonework came from the Baths of Caracalla and also the Colosseum. In the eighteenth century the palace was owned by the Bourbons and then by the French Republic. In 1936 it was given to the French government for 99 years and today is used as the French embassy.

Today it is possible to book tours of the palace. The Doric, Ionic and Corinthian pillars and forms are worth viewing as well as the gallery on the first floor with the fresco the *Triumph of Love in the Universe* by Annibale Carracci.

From the Palazzo Farnese walk along Via Dei Baullari then turn right onto Piazza Campo de'Fiori and right again for the Campo de'Fiori.

Piazza di Campo dei Fiori

The Campo dei Fiori translates as the *Field of Flowers* and is located where the Temple of Venus Victrix once stood attached to the Theatre of Pompey in ancient Rome.

Being so near to the River Tiber the area often flooded and fell into neglect. The flowers that grew on the waste land may have given rise to its name. In the fifteenth century Pope Callistus III organised the renovation of the area with a number of elegant palaces such as the Orsini Palace and the Palazzo della Cancelleria. The square was paved and soon became a place where prominent figures socialised.

Soon the area became the centre of a thriving horse market on Mondays and Saturdays and more buildings were constructed with artists' workshops and places to stay. The Piazza also became a place where executions were performed. Standing in the centre today is a statue of Giordano Bruno, a Dominican monk and philosopher, who was burned alive as a heretic.

Today except on Sundays there is a daily market selling fresh produce, meat, fish, flowers and spices. It is still a meeting point with its restaurants and cafes where people can eat and drink during the day and the evening.

Fontana della Terrina

A fountain designed and built by Giacomo della Porta was placed in the Campo dei Fiori in 1590 to provide access to water from the Aqua Virgo aqueduct. Because it resembled a tureen it became known as the *Fontana della Terrina*. The fountain stood in the middle of the market and rubbish was often thrown into it from the market stalls so a lid was put upon the fountain.

To make room for the statue of Giordano Bruno to be erected in the square the fountain was moved to the Piazza della Chiesa Nova and a copy without a lid was made and located on the west of the square.

From the Campo de'Fiori walk north-west towards Via Dei Baullari. After 55 metres turn right and continue onto Piazza della Cancelleria and the Palazzo Cancelleria will be on the left.

Palazzo della Cancelleria

The Renaissance Palace of the Chancellery commissioned by Cardinal Riaro and designed by Andrea Bregno and Bramante was built in in 1483. It later became the seat of government for the Papal States.

Like many other buildings in Rome the main facade is made from travertine taken from the Colosseum and considered by many to be a masterpiece of Renaissance architecture.

Inside is the *Hall of 100 Days* which is the courtroom said to have been painted by Vasari in 100 days. The remains of the fourth century Basilica di San Lorenzo in Damasco which is one of Rome's oldest churches can be seen in the courtyard.

From the Palazzo Cancelleria continue north on Piazza della Cancelleria and turn right onto Corso Vittorio Emanuel II then make a slight left onto Largo di Torre Argentina. After 50 metres turn right to stay on this road and then left again. The Largo di Torre Argentina will be on the right.

Largo di Torre Argentina

The Largo di Torre Argentina also known as the Area Sacra dell'Argentina is the Republican Forum that contains the remains of four ancient Roman temples and Pompey's theatre. The Republican Forum was discovered during demolition work during 1926 and originally the temples were named as four letters of the alphabet.

Temple A is the *Temple of Juturna* believed to have been built by Gaius Lutatius Catulus after his victory against the Carthaginians in 241 BC. It is hexagonal in shape and surrounded by a row of single columns similar to the style of temples built in ancient Greece. It was later used as a church and its apse is still visible.

Temple B is known as the *Temple of the Fortune of this Day* and was built by Quintus Lutatius Catulus in 101 BC. The circular temple has a flight of steps leading up to the altar and six Corinthian columns remain. The colossal statue of the goddess that was found here can be seen in the Capitoline museum.

Largo di Torre Argentina

Temple C was dedicated to Feronia the goddess of Fertility and thought to be the oldest temple. After the fire of 80 BC the temple was restored with black and white mosaics.

Temple D is the largest of the temples and dates from the second century BC with parts still buried under the modern street Via Florida.

Although the remains of Pompey's Theatre are located on this site little can be seen and most of the remains have been incorporated into nearby buildings. It was here that Julius Caesar was assassinated.

> *From the Largo di Torre Argentina walk along Corso Vittorio Emanuel II and turn right onto Piazza del Gesù. The Chiesa Gesù will be on the left.*

Chiesa del Santissimo Nome di Gesù

The Baroque Church of the Most Holy Name of Jesus is the world's oldest Jesuit church. The Jesuits were an order founded by Ignatius of Loyola. Michelangelo designed the first plans and the Duke of Gandia funded the construction of the church but due to papal opposition building stopped.

When Ignatius of Loyola died Giacomo Barozzi da Vignola and Giacomo della Porta became the main architects and building was funded by Cardinal Alessandro Farnese, grandson of Pope Paul III, then consecrated in 1568.

The interior of the church is adorned with rich jewellery, gilding, marble, sculptures, statues and frescos. The *Triumph of the Name of Jesus* ceiling fresco by Giovanni Battista Gaulli is impressive. Frescos and paintings of the passion of Jesus are portrayed by artists such as Giuseppe Valeriani and Gaspare Celio in the Chapel of Passion.

The painting of the *Madonna della Strada*, patron of the Jesuits, is an image of the Virgin Mary that hangs between the altars of Saint Ignatius and the Altar of the Holy Name of Jesus. The remains of Saint Ignatius rest in the left transept under his altar that was built by Jesuit Andrea Pozzo.

From the Chiesa del Gesù walk north-west on the Via del Gesù and turn left onto Via di Santa Caterina da Siena. Continue onto Piazza della Minerva where you will see the Obelisco della Minerva then turn right and the Chiesa Santa Maria Sopra Minerva will be on the right.

Pulcino della Minerva

The Elephant and Minerva Obelisk stands in the centre of the Piazza della Minerva. It was created in 1667 by Bernini and his assistant. The elephant forms the support base for the obelisk. This is the shortest Egyptian obelisk in Rome and is thought to have come from Sais.

Chiesa Santa Maria Sopra Minerva

The Church of Saint Mary over Minerva derives its name because it was built directly over the temple of Minerva. It was built in the thirteenth century but has been modified a number of times over the centuries.

This is the only Gothic church in Rome and was designed by Fra Sisto Fiorentino and Fra Ristoro da Campi. The colourful church has some interesting sights which include a number of tombs. Four popes are buried within the church. Below the main altar the patron saint of Italy, Catherine of Siena, is buried; minus her head. This is in the Basilica of San Domenico in Siena. Her tomb has an effigy sculptured by Isaia of Pisa in 1430.

In the Frangipane Chapel located to the left of the altar the painter Fra Angelico is buried. The Carafa chapel has frescos created by Filippino Lippi such as the *Triumph of Thomas of Aquino over the Heretics.*

The Cristo della Minerva is a marble sculpture of Christ carrying the cross crated by Michelangelo. It can be seen to the right of the main altar.

The Dome of San Pietro

Final Thoughts

These tours were written in response to guided tours that the author attended whilst in Rome, all of which tended to rush the participants from one location to the next. Hopefully you have enjoyed the five tours described in this book which, in contrast, should have allowed you to spend more time in the locations that you find most interesting.

There may not be time to explore the interior of every building or visit all museums included in each day's walking tour so a section for your own notes is included over the next few pages. Here you may wish to make notes of places to visit if you have any spare time on another day, or intend to return to Rome in the future. You may also wish to write down things such as restaurants or favourite attractions that you can pass onto friends.

Notes

Notes

Notes

NOTES

You may also enjoy reading...

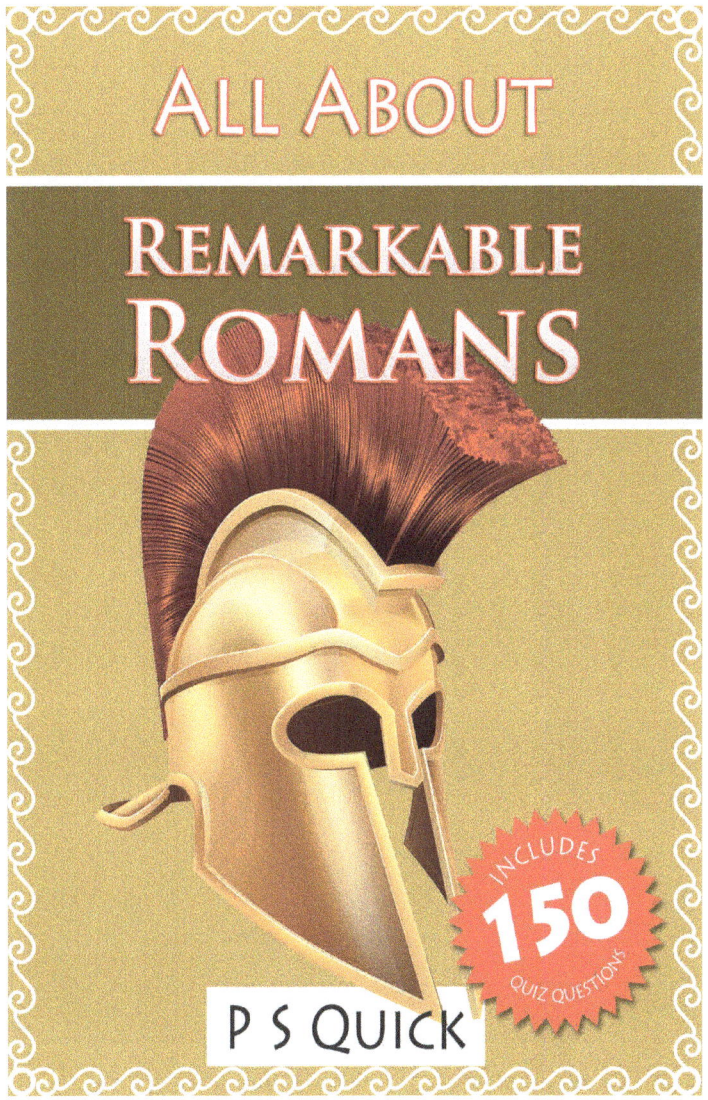

All About

Glorious Greeks

P S QUICK

INCLUDES **150** QUIZ QUESTIONS